Always a Bridesmaid

Always a Bridesmaid

89 Ways to Recycle That Bridesmaid Dress

Rebecca Whitlinger

**Andrews McMeel
Publishing**

Kansas City

www.andrewsmcmeel.com

99 00 01 02 03 LEO 10 9 8 7 6 5 4 3 2 1

Library of Congress Cataloging-in-Publication Data

Whitlinger, Rebecca.
    Always a bridesmaid : 89 ways to recycle that bridesmaid dress / Rebecca Whitlinger.
        p.   cm.
    ISBN 0-8362-8344-9
    1. Wedding costume—United States. 2. Wedding attendants—Costume—United States—
        Humor. I. Title.
    GT1753.U6W55 1999
    392.5'4—dc21

                                    98-31858
                                      CIP

Designed by Holly Camerlinck

Dedication

This book is dedicated to my beloved
parents, Hamilton and Helen
Whitlinger; Betty and Sidney Caslake;
best friend, Patricia Bilock Iannotta;
longtime editor, Kimberly Flaherty; *all* of
my treasured family members including
the Hanks, Haseltines, and Whitlingers;
Nicole Miller; Gary and Venetia Torre;
and most especially to my future
husband . . . whoever he may be!

☰ BURGER KING FRANCHISEE CANCER CARING CENTER ◈

A portion of my proceeds will be donated to the above, an agency providing free support services to cancer patients and families in Western Pennsylvania. If you would like to know more about this nonprofit group, check out their Web site: http://trfn.clpgh.org/cancercaring

Special thanks to all photographers including Archie Carpenter, Bob George of Pittsburgh Custom Darkroom, Splash Water Sports, Matt Bulvony, the Bedillions, and Hamilton Whitlinger.

Introduction

"You can wear it again." It's an acceptable little white lie echoed by brides throughout the land to their loyal contingent of bridesmaids. Yeah, right! Try showing up in an oddly hued creation complete with one if not all of the following—gargantuan butt bow, superfluous fabric (particularly in the posterior), satiny dyed-to-match shoes, appalling accessories (crocheted gloves, parasols, floppy hats)—and say with a sartorially straight face, "It's *not* from a wedding."

Not to mention the fact that many of your friends have seen this memorable outfit (and may in fact own one just like it)! Cutting it off at the knees really only alters the length; telltale details still scream *bridesmaid*.

Being a member of the wedding is a kooky rite of style passage, an occasion that blithely ignores fashion etiquette by featuring *matching* outfits (a fashion *don't* in any other circumstance) that are doomed to grace only the back of the closet, flouting the entire recycling age. Essentially, a bridesmaid dress is a lot like a cheerleading outfit: When removed from its one appropriate venue it, um, sticks out.

During my adult life, I've been privileged to be a bridesmaid in a half-dozen weddings. In 1988, I wore a gold sequin and gold lamé gown in a candlelight wedding. The dress assumed a regal and impressive glow from the evening festivities. But, like other gowns of its ilk, it seemed destined for permanent storage. However, gold *is* my favorite color. For fun, I decided to create an opportunity to wear it again. Inspired by a then-recent amateur photography course, I chose a picturesque demolition site near my house (that coincidentally featured a plethora of attractive construction workers). My best friend Patty Bilock, also a member of the gold dress wedding, agreed to snap the shot. When the pictures were developed, I literally caught gold fever and began scouting new locations. Patty rescued her gold dress from a storage trunk and started joining me in this innocuous spoof of a wedding tradition.

We relied on passersby, respective boyfriends, and friends to document the adventures on film. People would frequently ask why we were dressed up and our explanation always elicited laughter. These interactions proved what we knew to be true: The bridesmaid's plight is a universal theme. Even fashion clueless men could acknowledge the existence of these forgotten dresses possessed by their wives or girlfriends.

Separately and together, we have documented the fact that if you can't wear it anywhere, wear it *everywhere* and take the pictures to prove it. Sometimes, it is overwhelmingly embarrassing to appear in public because of the attention we inevitably attract, even though that's part of the purpose. However, it's the juxtaposition of the formal gown with ordinary circumstances that produces the best picture. We've become adept at throwing the dresses over our street clothes for a quick pic and even quicker getaway.

Keen observers immediately notice the distinctive difference between our two dresses. Patty's features a solid sequin front and open back; mine is off the shoulder. While my gown is remarkably durable considering what it has been subjected to, a spare dress was just the insurance I needed. I acquired a "double" to Patty's from another bridesmaid. Honestly, a girl just can't own enough sequins, particularly now that I regularly receive letters requesting a sample sequin from my famous frock and invitations from people I've never met to attend events and weddings.

After we won the Funniest Pittsburghers contest in 1991 for "outing" the dresses (admittedly there was a dearth of applicants and unfortunately no prize), I then started pitching the story to national publications. Soon after, Patty and I wearing the dresses were featured in *Redbook* magazine and the *Chicago Tribune*. For me, it was an unusual premise as a freelance fashion-and-health writer to be known for wearing the *same* dress so it's good I kept my day job as a fundraiser. I won a bridesmaid essay contest a couple of years ago and then later guested (very briefly) on *The Oprah Winfrey*

Show. Because I am not yet immersed in marriage and family life, I have more time to devote to this endeavor than Patty. A feature in a December 1997 issue of *People* magazine (including a full-page unflattering shot that caused tears for two weeks), followed by appearances on the *Today* show, *The Dini Show* (Toronto, Canada), and an article in A&E's *Biography Magazine* solidified plans for this book.

The concept of "once is not enough, wear it again" prompted me to create "Bridesmaids Revisited and the Men Who Love Them" for the Burger King Cancer Caring Center in Pittsburgh, Pennsylvania, where I am executive director. In June 1998, more than two hundred people attended this first annual benefit wearing something they never thought they would wear again. At this event, it was a real *compliment* for someone to say, "Gee, what an ugly dress!" A couple was legally joined in holy matrimony (and I was a bridesmaid!). A good time was had by all; translating my quirky hobby into a part of my job turned out to be pretty cool.

At the First Annual "Bridesmaids Revisited and the Men Who Love Them" in June 1998, the newly married Mr. and Mrs. Robert Smeyres are surrounded by the World's Largest Wedding Party.

Well, it's true that so far, "always a bridesmaid" does apply to me. I *do* look forward to getting married some day. After all, time is moving on. But I'm not panicking, mainly because I think guys can sense desperation the way dogs smell fear. I'm frequently asked what the bridesmaid gowns will look like for *my* wedding. The pageantry of weddings is important and I don't necessarily advocate changing the tradition (although I'm obviously not against it either). Rest assured, my Gold Dress will be *invited* to make a brief appearance . . . maybe at the reception. But definitely not on the honeymoon.

Imagine the possibilities and consider one or more of the tips for alternative uses listed throughout this book. While it may be considered drastic, some dresses can even be recycled by (gulp!) cutting them. Personally I couldn't dismember any of my dresses, but recognize everyone may not share the same attachment.

The First* Gold Dress Picture: I passed this site every day and thought it would provide an interesting opportunity to wear the dress again. Like a phoenix rising.

*Not counting the wedding.

Tip: Treat your gown as lovingly as a pair of old jeans. Rip at knees and just wear *everywhere.*

My personal campaign for a civic duty dress code went unnoticed; most poll workers assured me that formal attire was unnecessary. Darn! However, I must say the gold skirt peeking underneath that tired curtain was a fashion "do."

Warning: Prolonged exposure to sunlight while wearing gold may accelerate UV intensity. Sunglasses are a necessity due to the blinding glare from the golden sequins, so sunscreen was liberally applied.

Tip:
Fun in the sun—use your dress as a hammock and/or beach towel.

New York, New York, and
what a wonderful gown!

Tip:

Create
sumptuous
padded hangers
à la
Joan Crawford.

No one bet I could make this shot. And they were absolutely right. My game won't be improving anytime soon because I believe in avoiding all sports that entail bending over. It's not my best feature.

Tip:

Martha would
be proud.
Make napkins,
place mats,
tablecloths,
runners,
curtain tiebacks,
pillows,
seat covers,
lamp shades ...
you get the idea.

Cape Cod 1989: I flew to Boston to proudly serve as a bridesmaid when my brother Bob married Cyndi. About this time I realized the Gold Dress was as vital to pack as a toothbrush and a push-up bra.

Witness Patty's artful interpretation of "Gumby meets the Statue of Liberty." This character scared away Halloween pranksters (and, for that matter, crows and other flying creatures).

Tip:

Scarecrow outfit.

Patty and I traveled to Paris in 1989, allotting valuable and significant space in our suitcases for the gold gowns. We gleefully wore them for a snapshot under the Eiffel Tower. *Quel horreur!* The film was ruined (don't ask). This picture is our only surviving souvenir. I have already prepared for a return trip by posing for my passport picture wearing you-know-what.

Tip:

Vacation Bonus Tip: Yards of gold fabric serve as ideal cushion for breakables.

Tip:
Remove butt
bow and place
on wall
over favorite
artwork.

In Palm Beach, Florida, this monkey was all business as he gravitated toward tourists with dollar bills in their hands for Polaroid pictures. Two people thought that photos were available with *both* the monkey and the girl in the Gold Dress so I humbly cooperated.

We had plenty of ups and downs the day we rode Pittsburgh's Kennywood Park Thunderbolt roller coaster seven times for a pilot episode of *Redbook TV*, hosted by Maureen O'Boyle. They also filmed us horseback riding and working at Burger King.

Tip:

Balloon window shade–stuff with petticoat!

The eccentric apple doesn't fall far from the tree! My father, a strolling violinist, posed for his driver's license picture while wearing a tux. He's a "Ham" literally—his real name is Hamilton. So naturally, I followed his lead. However, with a photo like this, I'll probably *always* be a bridesmaid. Or at least until my license expires.

Bargaining Point: Don't expect to get the price knocked down when you go antiquing in a formal gown.

Tip:

The verdict's in! Wear it while pleading temporary insanity for a parking violation.

Give to
deserving little
girl for dress-
up. Halloween.
prom, debutante
ball, etc.

If not affecting a ghostlike
persona on Halloween, I
appear as the perennial
favorite—"a member of a
wedding." Let's face it: a
bridesmaid dress is
nothing if not a costume.

The ticket taker at this tourist stop in Florida brightened considerably when I sought permission to "pet" the stuffed lion. He asked, "How much you gonna pay me?" I explained that the standard fee was a big fat zero. "Ya got two minutes and don't steal nothin'," he growled. Usually the Gold Dress has more of a taming effect on people.

Tip:

For a Christmas tree skirt, wrap around base for a festive holiday decoration. Plus: easily *un*wraps for unexpected photo op.

For a radio promotion, I was duct-taped to a pole in downtown Pittsburgh. Tape (a lot of it) was wrapped around my torso, substantially reducing my ability to breathe but creating the illusion of a wasplike waistline. They unceremoniously cut me down when my face started to turn blue.

Toronto: I like the concept of communing with fish ... without getting wet!

Tip:

Outfit your cat, dog, or other beloved pet. Fish not recommended.

Tip:

Store in car trunk for emergencies; could eventually replace white distress flag!

The perfect illustration of why I keep my dress in the trunk at all times. You just never know when a photo op will present itself. I always wanted a picture by a train but my preference would have been a more exotic location than Ohio. No offense intended to the Buckeye state.

Tip:
Impersonate visiting royalty. Lucy Ricardo did it on *I Love Lucy*.

We would have preferred visiting the Taj Mahal in India but budgetary considerations dictated the Atlantic City casino.

Formal attire for a lawn party is a capital idea! Patty and I visited my cousins Leslie and Pam in Washington, D.C., right after *Redbook* magazine came out in 1993. Several people recognized us, but sadly, all were women. Happily, the reverse was true when we won a local Funniest Pittsburghers contest. I received letters, flowers, and chocolates (regrettably a personal favorite) from several local men, much to the extreme annoyance of my then-boyfriend who did not agree with me that platonically pursuing new friendships with the senders would provide amusing party conversation.

Tip:

Paint drop
cloth.
Caution:
slippery
when wet.

Uncharacteristically subdued as a guest on *The Oprah Winfrey Show*, it did
not occur to me to pose with Oprah or even just under this sign. Next time.
Oprah inquired if I wore the dress on dates. Naturally I said yes and she
asked if the guys ever called again. Hmmm. Maybe *that's* the problem. (Do
you think this book could qualify for her reading club?)

Tip:

Be different— wear for Casual Day at the office.

Just another working stiff.

Because of my association with the Burger King Cancer Caring Center, a couple of franchisees claim they would hire me if I ever decide to moonlight. There's only one problem—that troublesome issue of uniforms. Guess what I want to wear! Frankly, I'm interested in conducting a scientific experiment. If I actually ate all the french fries I wanted, would I eventually grow tired of them?

Pittsburgh's "You Gotta Regatta": The main reason for our crossed arms is that it was just too criminally early in the morning and we were cranky. My sailorlike cap added authentic flavor to the festivities. It also partially concealed some bad A.M. hair.

Tip:

Give it away!
Donate to a
charity store.
May be tax-
deductible.

Patty made points
by going for the
gold at a charity
volleyball game.

Although she's never shot more than a water pistol, Patty wasn't gun-shy about combining a quilted camouflage vest with a gold skirt.

Tip:
Give neighbors a kick. Hang on clothesline to enliven otherwise mundane laundry.

I saw this character from the other side of the road and begged my then-boyfriend to pull over and take this picture. At this point, he (my boyfriend) literally wanted to shoot me, so he did. I later carefully cut out my silhouette and this character and glued us on postcards of crowded beaches and mailed them to dozens of friends, sort of like a "Where's Waldo?" type thing.

Tip:

Qualify for High Occupancy Vehicle lane. Dress mannequin and place in passenger seat. Note: State laws vary. May be illegal.

Hit the deck! For us, white-water rafting is infinitely more appealing when executed on land.

Tip:

Start an all-girl karaoke group with other bridesmaids from the wedding party.

Always a Bridesmaid   27

Twenty degrees below
zero dictated long
underwear and winter
coats for our audience
with Punxsutawney Phil,
the groundhog
prognosticator. I presented
him with a souvenir
sequin but he seemed
unimpressed. Typical male!

I'd rather be overdressed than underdressed for every occasion. Additional fashion statement—white Lucite purse!

Tip:

The perfect Mardi Gras outfit.

Later, while in the boat at this Florida alligator farm, I noticed with some trepidation that the live alligators were attracted to sequins. Of course, the fact that I was dangling the spare Gold Dress much like a red flag in front of a bull and reprising a mating call I heard in a Tarzan of the Apes movie did not help.

Although we were bushed, it just wouldn't have been prudent to leave Washington, D.C., without this unparalleled tête-à-tête fete! Some readers may conclude that the middle figure is actually a cardboard cutout and, well, they're right.

Tip:

Be optimistic. Save for millennium version of *Let's Make a Deal.*

Tackling the runway with Pittsburgh Steelers escorts Troy Sadowski and Norm Johnson at the Pittsburgh Steelers Fashion Show benefiting the Cancer Caring Center. Fearing an audience stampede, I insisted that the emcees stress that my dress was in no way, shape, or form for sale.

Strike a pose:
We couldn't
proceed down the
aisle on Patty's
wedding day in
1996 without a
gold candid,
complete with
Honorary Gold Dress
Girl Beth Bilock
(Patty's sister). I
loved the regal title of
Maid of Honor
(although Spinster of
Honor has a distinctive
ring)!

Sure, these dresses were elegant but nothing can or will ever compare to the Gold Dress.

Tip:

Start fun new tradition—mail to bride on first anniversary. Enclose a note: "Maybe *you* can wear this."

It's no small feat to climb a ladder in a flammable gown. *Bonus:* Cute firemen!

Tip:
Divorce party bonfire. Reminder: Most dresses are *not* flame-retardant. Add marshmallows.

Inside the CN Tower in Toronto, I felt dizzier than usual as I surveyed the spectacular view as filmed by *The Dini Show*. Unfortunately, the camera lighting created a rather luteous gluteus maximus!

Tip:

Keep it! Plan your own "Bridesmaids Revisited" benefit for a worthy cause. Invite me—I'd love to attend.

Slippery frippery: Because the Gold Dress is showered with attention, it seemed appropriate to finally attempt to clean it. The water's magical properties rejuvenated the gold luster, insuring a plethora of future wearings.

Tip:

Decorative sling cover for broken arm.

Florida, 1998: A day without the Gold Dress is like a day without sunshine!

Tip:
Garden "tulle"–cover plants to protect from frost.

Virtually the
only pleasant reminder of one ex-
boyfriend is this photo he took of my parasailing odyssey in
Cancun, Mexico. Initially, I was a bit miffed that the life jacket eclipsed the
sequin top but once in the air, I appreciated any and all safety measures.
Lamé is slippery and I briefly felt this could be the end of the golden years.

The Pittsburgh Steelers graciously lowered their steel curtain
and allowed us into the locker room, which was expectedly
replete with athletic gear in general and footwear in
particular. Although they may not be state-of-the-art, I still
prefer my gold hightops.

For some inexplicable reason, I told *Today* show coanchor Matt Lauer to look mad and being a congenial host, he complied. Katie Couric intended to interview me while actually wearing one of her old bridesmaid dresses but couldn't retrieve it from her parents' house in time.

Proud as a peacock.

Tip:

Blind Date
Attire.
If you *like* the
guy, tell him
you just came
from a wedding.
If you *don't* like
him, scare him
off with, "Why
waste time? I
know a nice
justice of the
peace."

NBC
STUDIO 1A
35 West 48th Street
New York, New York.

Meeting weatherman
Willard Scott was a
breeze and I'm glad I
didn't have to wait till
my hundredth
birthday!

Tip:

Ideal gift for drag queen—glam-drag rules!

Holiday 1997: Another humbling picture—the goggles are an uncanny double of the protective glasses worn in seventh-grade science class. The dress was unscathed. In fact, I could breathe easier upon seeing that water enhanced the splendor.

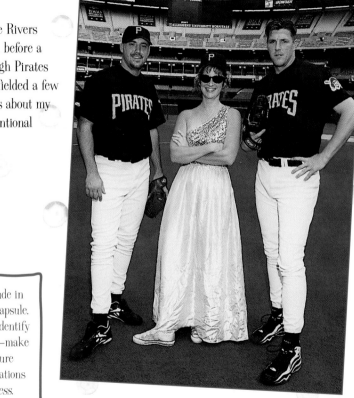

At Three Rivers Stadium before a Pittsburgh Pirates game, I fielded a few inquiries about my unconventional uniform.

Tip:
Include in time capsule. Don't identify origin—make future generations *guess*.

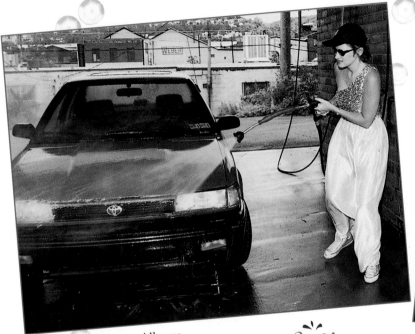

Cleanliness is next to goldliness.

Tip:

Tea kettle cozy.
For that matter,
vacuum cleaner
cozy.

The Gold Dress provided the perfect counterpoint to formal wear showcased by members of the renowned Pittsburgh Symphony Orchestra.

When I'm out
in the Dress, I
never cross the
line. . . .

Your suggestions and adventures . . .
Please send to: The Gold Dress Bridesmaid
c/o Andrews McMeel Publishing, 4520 Main Street, Kansas City, MO 64111-7701.
Or e-mail bridesmaid@amuniversal.com
Send a SASE for a gold sequin.